MYRIADS OF FLOWERS

See page 41

See page 42

See page 43

See page 44

See page 45

See page 47

See page 48

See page 49

See page 50

See page 51

See page 52

See page 53

 # BOUQUETS

See page 55

See page 57

18 See page 58

See page 59

See page 60

  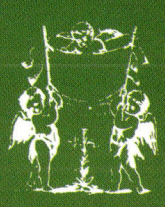

FLOWERS IN SEASON

WINTER

SPRING

SUMMER

AUTUMN

See page 61

See page 62

See page 63

See page 65

See page 66

See page 67.

See page 68

See page 69

THE ALPHABETS

See page 70

See page 71

GENERAL INFORMATION ON EMBROIDERY

BASIC STITCHES

RUNNING STITCH	DARNING STITCH	BACK STITCH
OUTLINE STITCH	CHAIN STITCH	BROKEN CHAIN STITCH
	TWISTED CHAIN STITCH	THE NEEDLE IS INSERTED OUTSIDE THE PRECEEDING LOOP.
COUCHING STITCH		DOUBLE CHAIN STITCH
RUMANIAN STITCH	RUMANIAN COUCHING STITCH	HERRING-BONE STITCH
STRAIGHT STITCH	HERRING-BONE STITCH VARIATION	CLOSED HERRING-BONE STITCH
	A NEW THREAD IS CAST OVER THE HERRING-BONE STITCH.	THE TOP AND BOTTOM OF THE STITCH ARE CLOSED.

CROSS STITCH

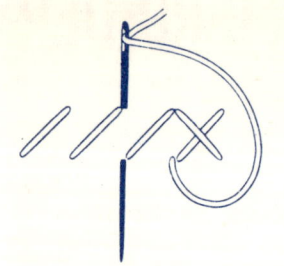

BUTTONHOLE STITCH

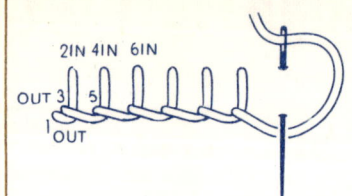

CLOSED BUTTONHOLE STITCH

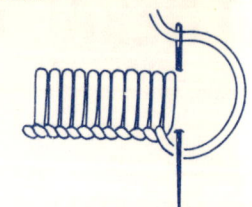

DOUBLE CROSS STITCH

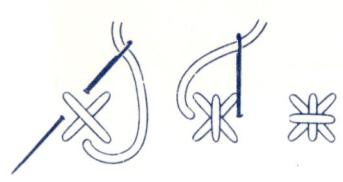

BUTTONHOLE SCALLOP

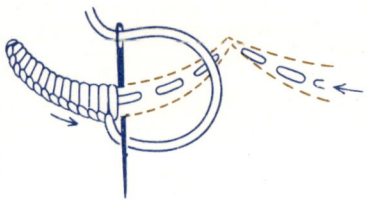

CLOSED BUTTONHOLE STITCH IS MADE OVER THE AUXILIARY RUNNING STITCHES. THE FABRIC IS TO BE THEN TRIMMED OFF THE SCALLOPS.

TAILLOR'S BUTTONHOLE STITCH

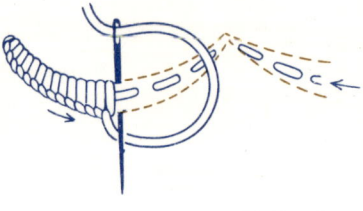

MADE IN THE SAME WAY AS IN CASE OF BUTTONHOLE STITCH, WITH THE BOTTOM KNOTTED.

SATIN STITCH

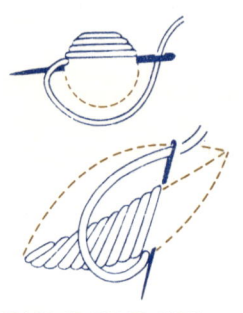

THE SPACE IS FILLED WITH STRAIGHT STITCH. THE LEAF IS MADE SYMMETRICALLY FROM THE CENTER LINE.

PADDED SATIN STITCH

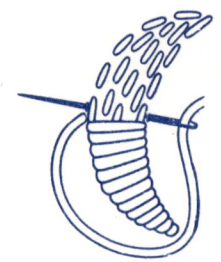

THE SPACE IS FILLED WITH RUNNING STITCH, BEFORE SATIN STITCH IS MADE OVER.

LONG AND SHORT STITCH

LONG AND SHORT STITCHES ARE MADE REGULARLY OR IRREGULARLY

CORAL STITCH

FRENCH KNOT (STITCH)

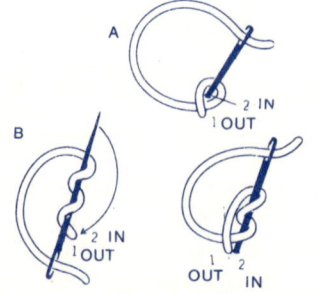

FRENCH KNOT VARIATION

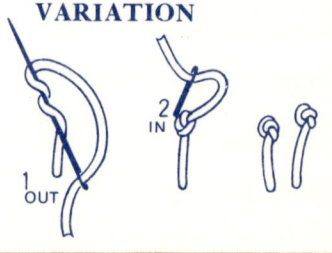

GERMAN KNOT (STITCH)

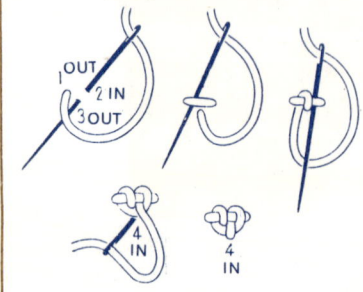

MACRAMÉ STITCH

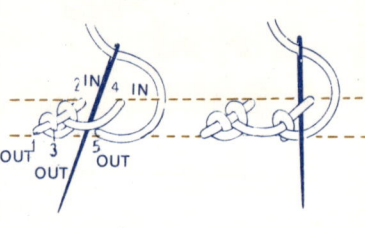

FLY STITCH

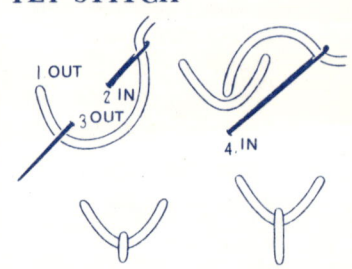

FERN STITCH

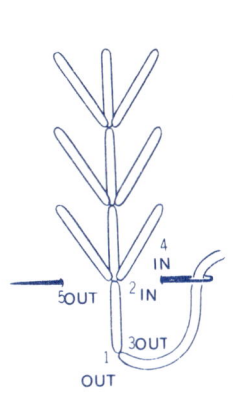

FEATHER STITCH

INSERT THE NEEDLE STRAIGHT AS SHOWN BY 2-3, 4-5.

DOUBLE FEATHER STITCH

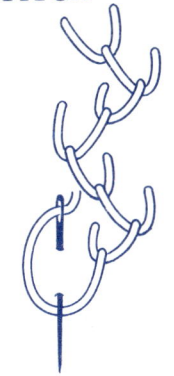

FEATHER STITCH, TWO BY TWO IN THE SAME DIRECTION.

BULLION STITCH

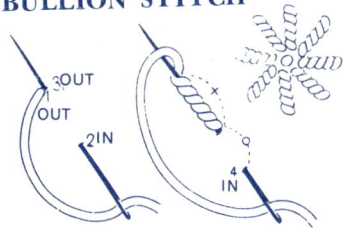

BULLIONKNOT STITCH

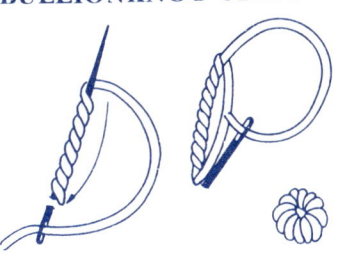

FERN STITCH VARIATION

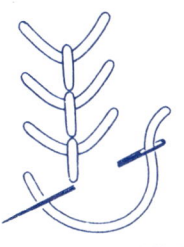

BULLION CHAIN STITCH

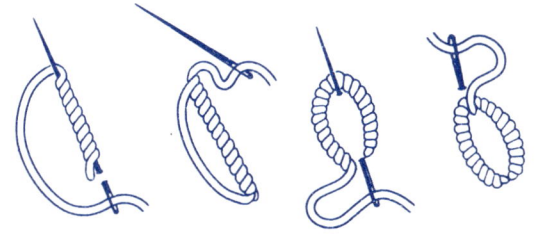

THE NEEDLE, AFTER EMERGED, TAKES UP A FEW THREADS OF THE FABRIC, THEN IS CAST ROUND BY THE STITCHING THREAD AS LONG AS REQUIRED. IT THEN SLIPS OUT OF THE COILED LOOP, AND IS FIXED NEXT TO THE STARTING POINT, FORMING A RING, TO BE THEN FASTENED WITH A LAZY DAISY STITCH.

CHAIN FILLING STITCH

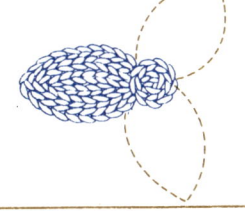

FRENCH KNOT FILLING STITCH

THE SPACE IS FILLED WITH FRENCH KNOTS.

RANDOM CROSS STITCH

STITCHES ARE MADE IN ALL DIRECTIONS AT LIBERTY.

SEED FILLING STITCH

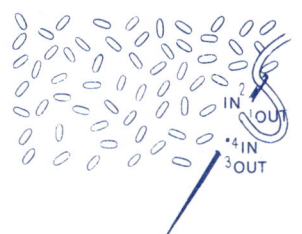

BUTTONHOLE FILLING STITCH

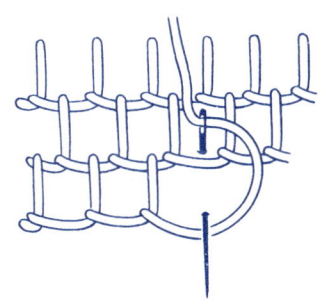

OPEN BUTTONHOLE FILLING STITCH

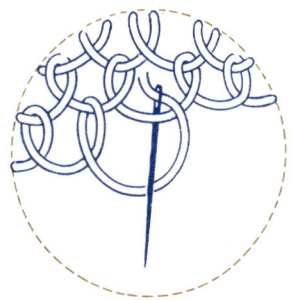

FIRST, FROM LEFT TO RIGHT, THEN FROM RIGHT TO LEFT, THE NEEDLE GOES SCOOPING THE LOOPS OF THE PREVIOUS ROW, WITHOUT BEING INSERTED TO THE FABIRC WHILE MAKING A ROW.

OUTLINE FILLING STITCH

CONTOUR THE SHAPE, AND FILL THE INSIDE WITH OUTLINE STITCHES.

LAZY DAISY STITCH
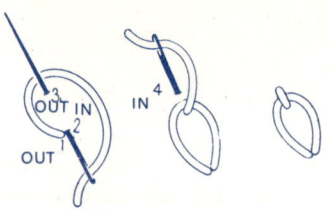

DOUBLE LAZY DAISY STITCH
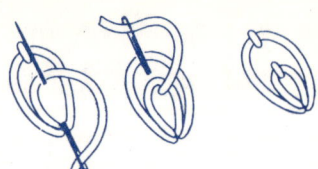

LAZY DAISY STITCH VARIATION
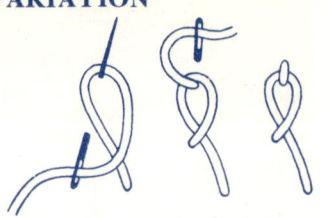

HOLBEIN STITCH

WORK THE RUNNING STITCH, THEN TRACE THE ROW FILLING THE SPACES OF THE STITCHES.

UNEVEN HOLBEIN STITCH
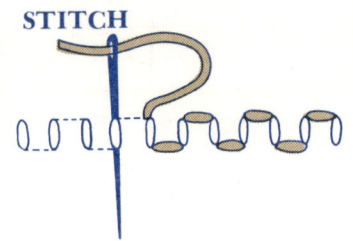

ZIGZAG STITCH
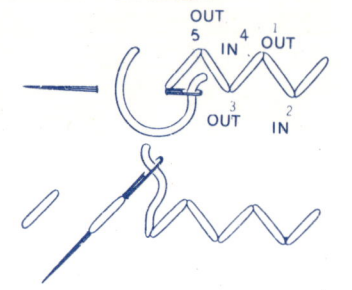

CABLE CHAIN STITCH

THREADED CHAIN STITCH
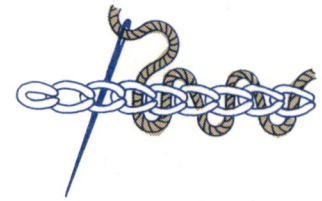

A SEPARATE THREAD IS PASSED THROUGH THE CHAIN STITCH.

WHIPPED CHAIN STITCH
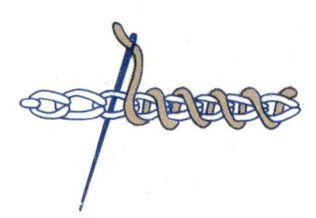

DOT STITCH

TWO SMALL BACK STITCHES ARE MADE ON THE SAME PLACE.

DOUBLE KNOT STITCH
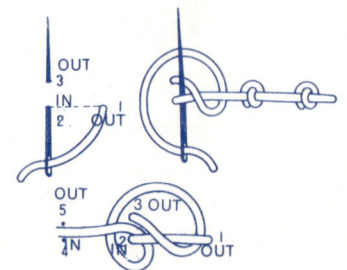

MADE IN THE SAME WAY AS IN CASE OF MACRAMÉ STITCH, BUT WORKED FROM RIGHT TO LEFT.

WHEAT SHEAF STITCH
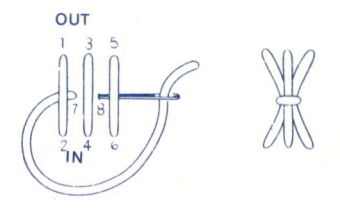

COUCHED TRELLIS STITCH
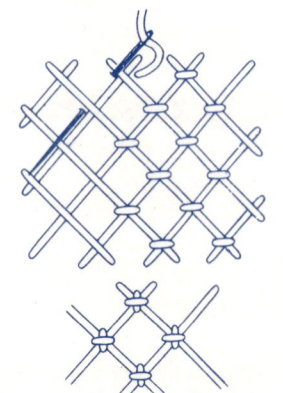

DIAGONAL PLAID IS CAUGHT AT CROSSING POINTS BY A SEPARATE THREAD.

ANTWERP EDGE
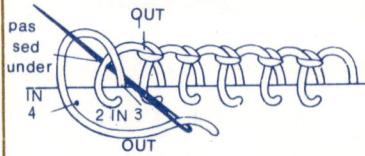

SURFACE DARNING STITCH
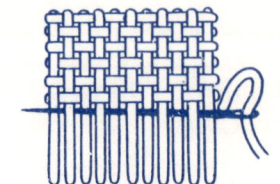

THREADS ARE PASSED VERTICALLY, THEN CROSSED BY HORIZONTAL DARNING STITCHES, WITHOUT INSERTING THE NEEDLE TO THE FABRIC.

WHIPPED BACK STITCH

SHADOW STITCH

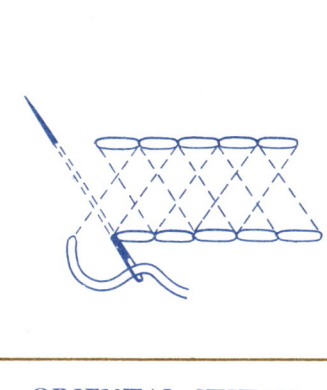

FLAT STITCH

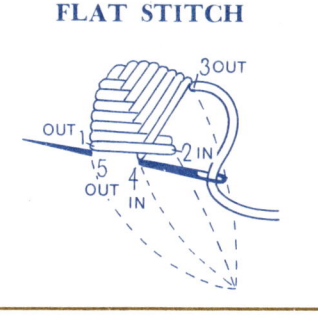

BUTTONHOLE STITCH VARIATION

LEAF STITCH

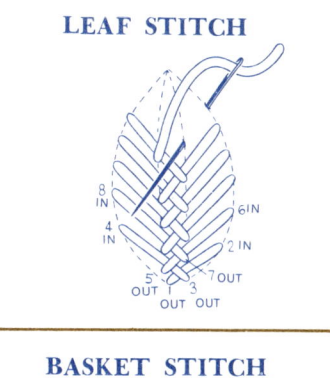

BUTTONHOLE SCALLOP VARIATION

ORIENTAL STITCH

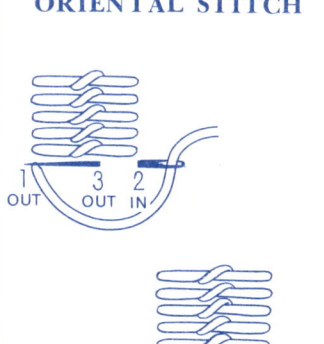

BASKET STITCH

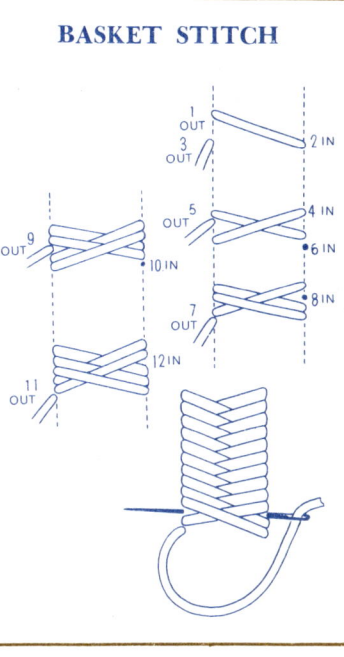

TWISTED CHAIN STITCH VARIATION

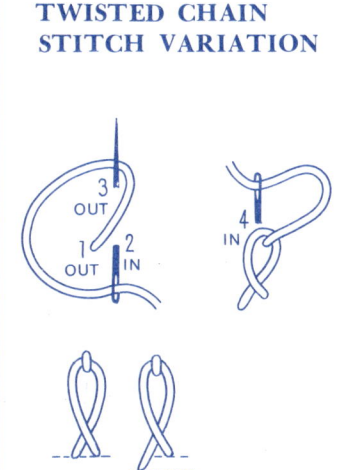

SINGLEKNOT STITCH

LONG & SHORT STITCH VARIATION

FISHBONE STITCH

BASKET FILLING STITCH

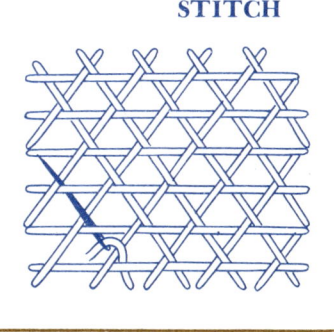

EMBROIDERY THREADS

THE MOST POPULAR FOR EMBROIDERY ARE Nos. 25 and 5.

#25—One thread consists of 6 strands, and measures 8m per skein. Yor can pull out as many threads as required from the bundle if necessary (according to the design).

#5—Single thick thread, and is quite lustrous. 1 skein measures 25m. Suitable for rough stitches.

Besides these, you have a wide variety of them such as cottons, rayons, silk, wools ... even metal threads. The sizes also range from thick, medium, fine and extreme fine.

✿ HANDLING THE THREAD

The threads Nos. 25, 5 and 4 come in a bundle or ball, depending on the manufacturer. When they are formed in a ring, untie the twist, and cut one end of the ring with scissors, and pull out one by one. When they are gathered together and held by one or two paper label/labels, pull out the length from the core of the bundle.

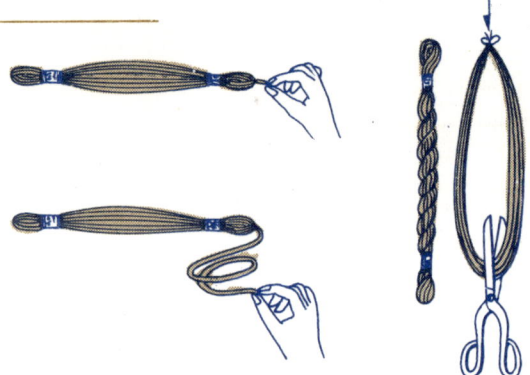

TIED WITH A THREAD

✿ PASSING THE THREAD THROUGH THE NEEDLE

When you pass 4 strands of the thread through an embroidery needle, fold the ends of the threads, and insert the folded edge through hole of the needle. (See illustration on right) Do the same way when you pass a thick yarn like wool.

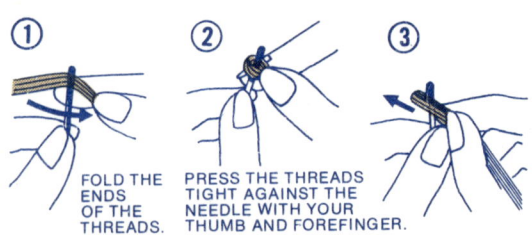

① FOLD THE ENDS OF THE THREADS.
② PRESS THE THREADS TIGHT AGAINST THE NEEDLE WITH YOUR THUMB AND FOREFINGER.

HINTS ON STITCHING

✿ HOW TO START AND END STITCHING

A securing knot is rarely made in embroidery. To start stitching, see the illustration below. If you need to make a knot, form a small loop round the needle, and gently pull out the needle, with your left thumb pressing the loop.

GENERAL STITCHING

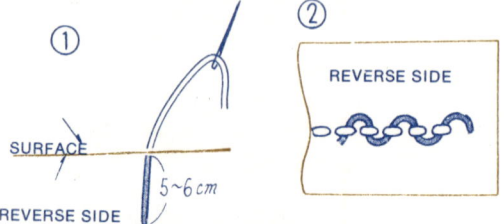

SEW THROUGH THE STITCHES ON THE WRONG SIDE (NOT SHOWING ON THE RIGHT SIDE), WHEN START OR END THE SEAM.

FILLING STITCHING

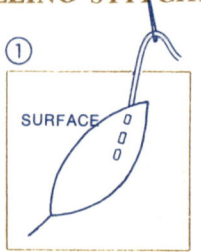
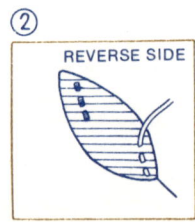

SEW A FEW STITCHES TOWARD THE STARTING POINT.

SEW BACK A FEW STITCHES BEFORE BREAKING OFF (CAREFULLY NOT TO SHOW THE SEAM ON FRONT).

HOW TO TRANSFER A DESIGN

Place a sheet of tracing paper over the design, and copy it drawing with a hard (lead) pencil.

❀ USING CARBON PAPER

Place the waxed side of the carbon which is produced for dressmaking, down on the right side of the material that's been pinned on a board. Put tracing paper over the carbon, and work round carefully with a pencil or a tracing wheel.

❀ USING A GLASS PLATE

Bridge two boxes with a piece of opaque glass (to minimize eye strain) and put a lighted bulb under the glass. Transfer a design found in book on tracing paper. Then put the tracing paper on the glass, lay the material thereon, and outline directly on the material with a hard pencil.

❀ USING TISSUE PAPER

Trace the design onto a sheet of smooth tissue paper, and tack this into position at the edges of the background material. Using a basting thread, tack around the whole of the design through the tissue paper and material. Embroider over it, then remove the paper.

ENLARGING THE DESIGN

Draw a graph with right squares over the design. The more complicated the design, the smaller the squares. Then draw in another piece of paper the squares that are enlarged at regular rate, and trace the design in the enlarged graph. Do contrary when reducing the design.

NEEDLLEWORK on page cover *3 strands.*

NEEDLLEWORK on page 1. *3 strands.*

NEEDLLEWORK on page 2. *3 strands.*

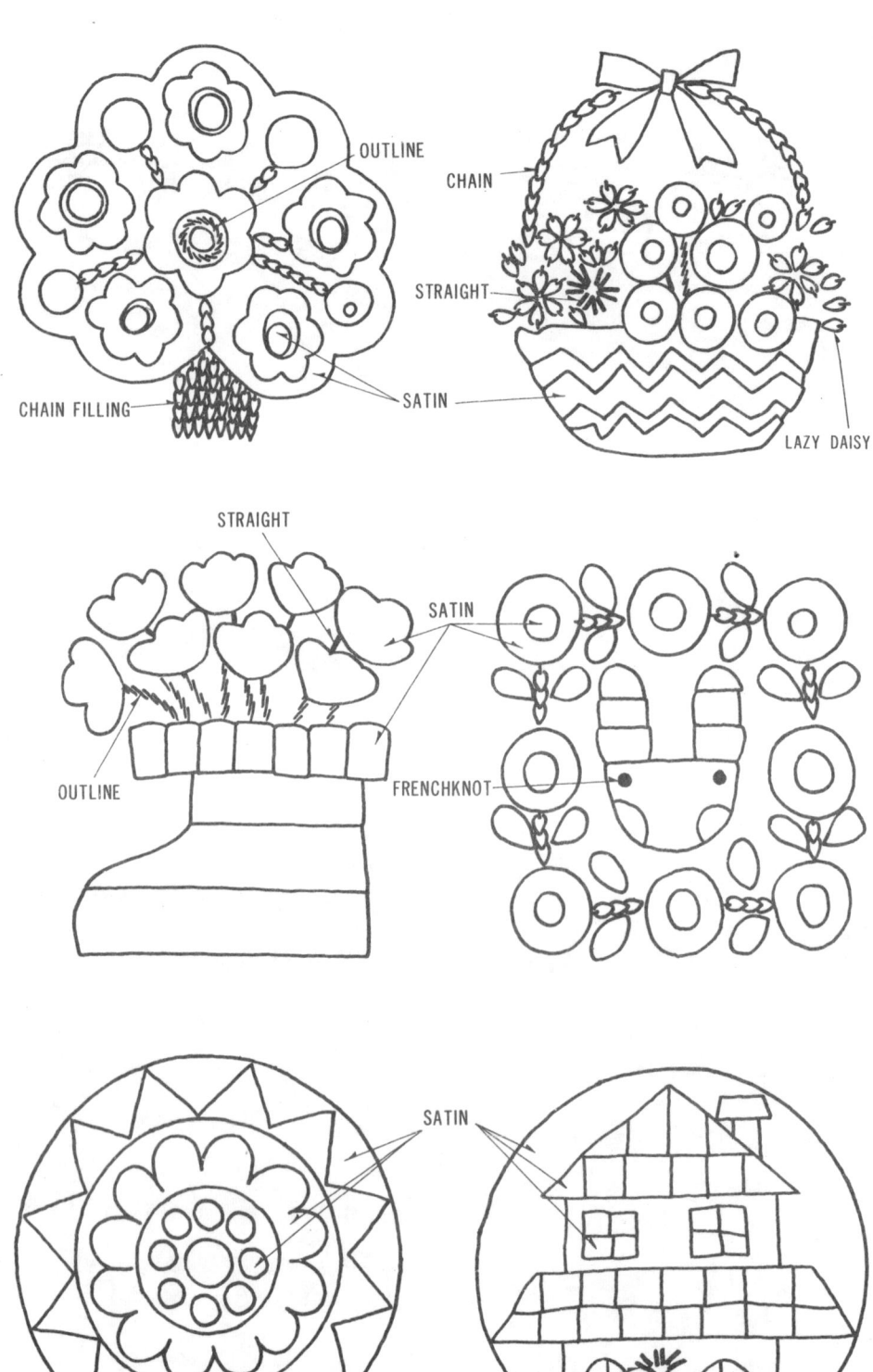

NEEDLLEWORK on page 3.   *3 strands.*

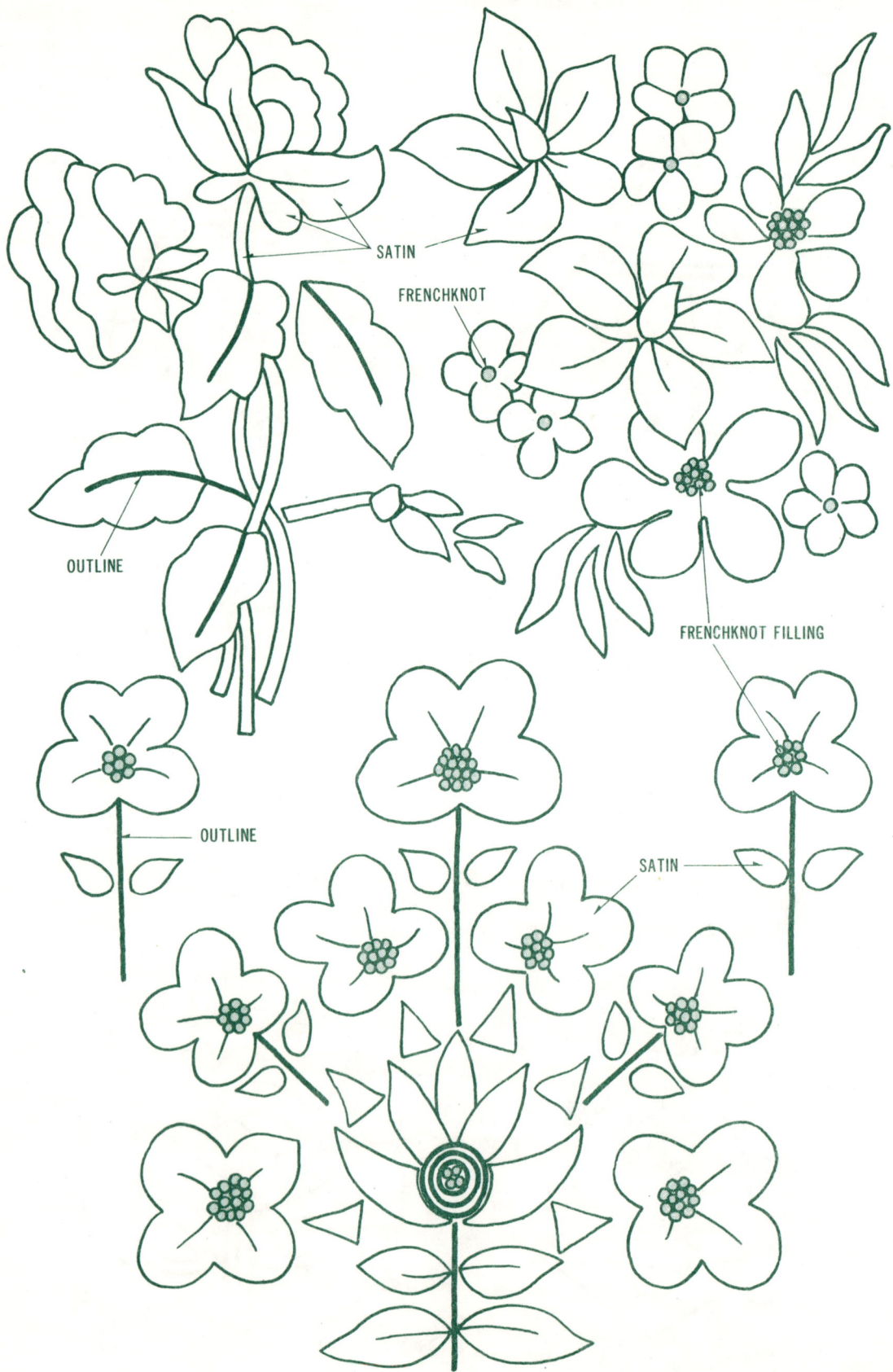

NEEDLLEWORK on page 5.   *3 strands except appointment.*

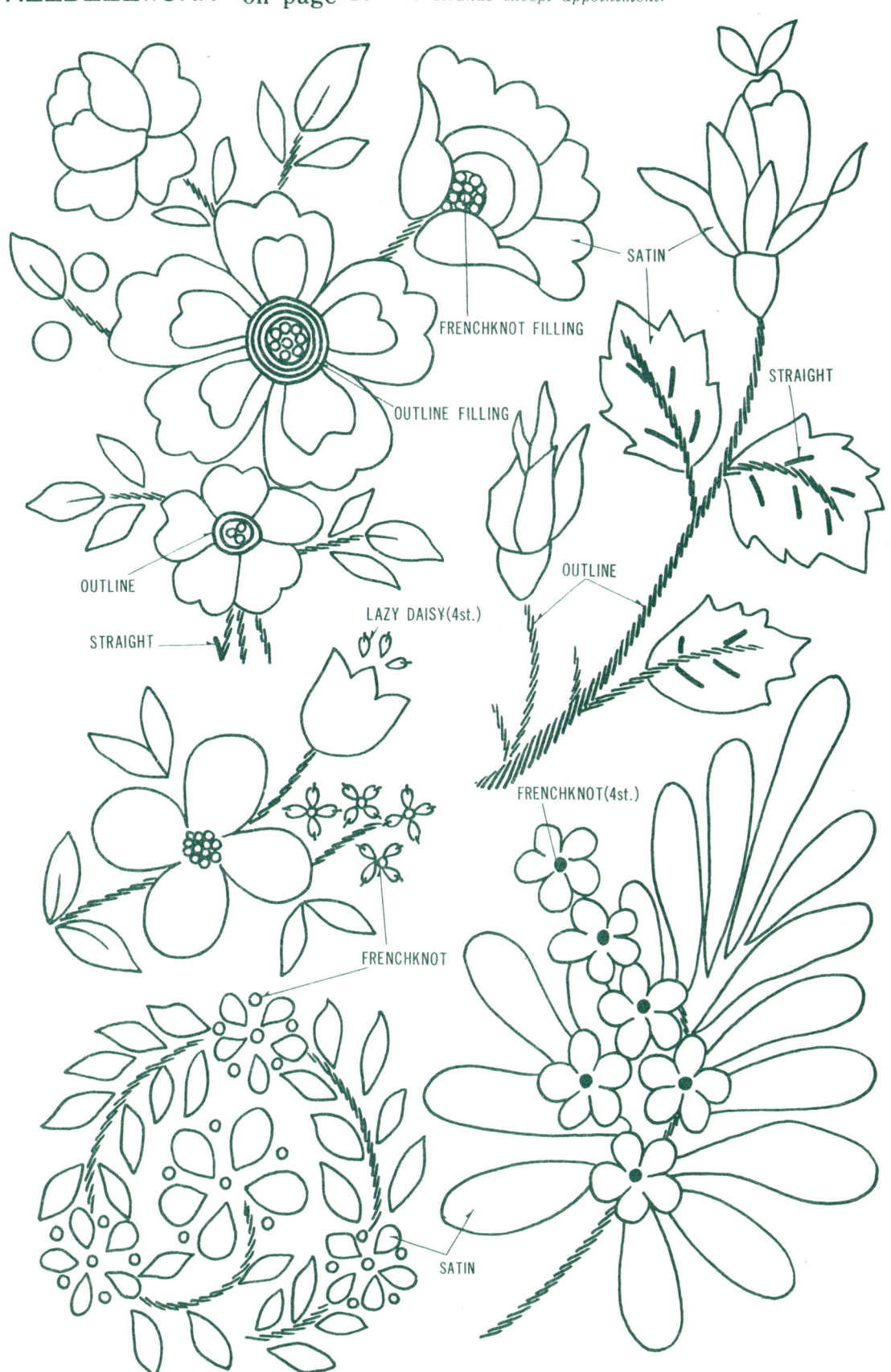

NEEDLLEWORK on page 7. *2 strands.*

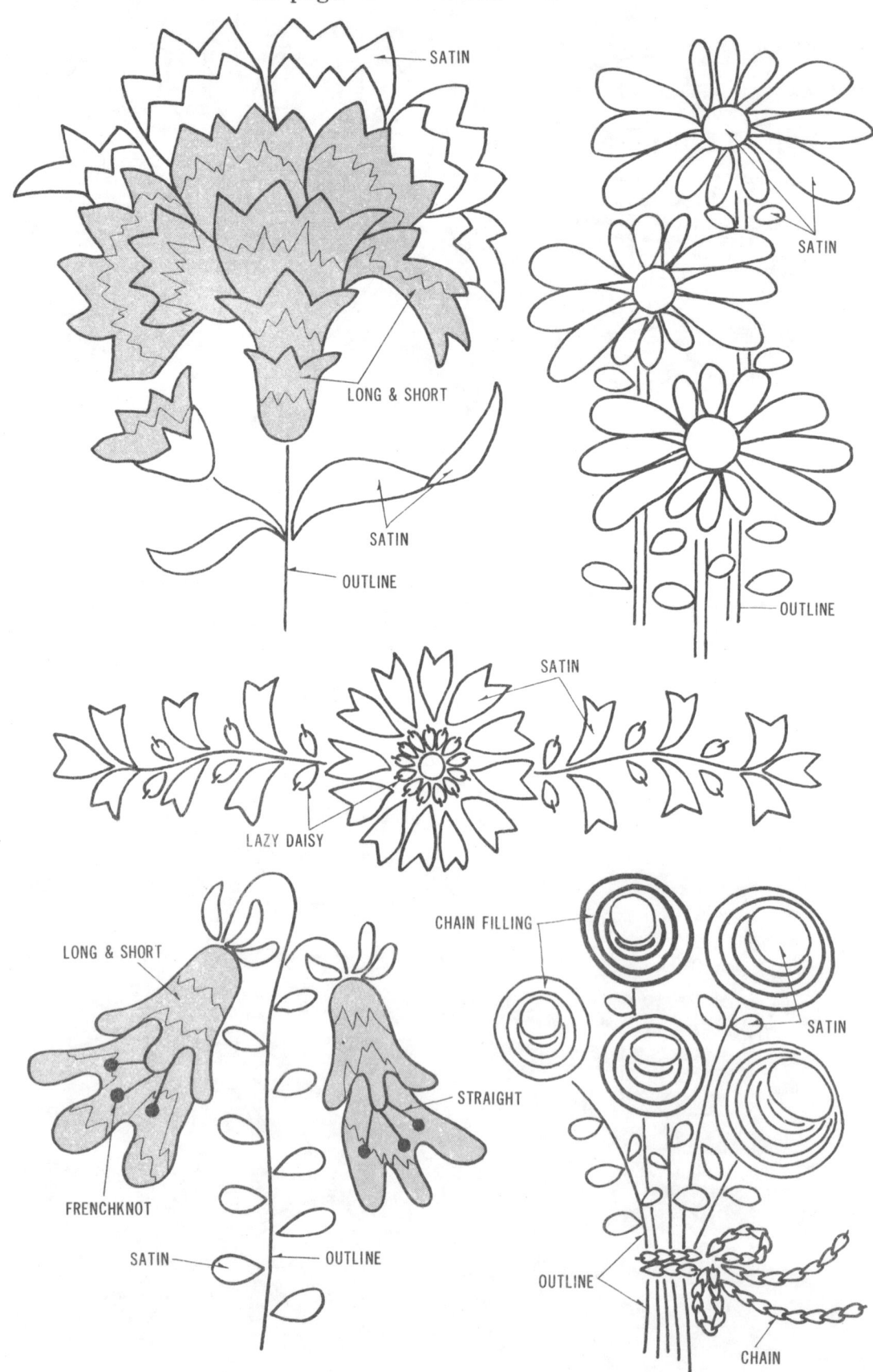

NEEDLLEWORK on page 9. *4 strands*

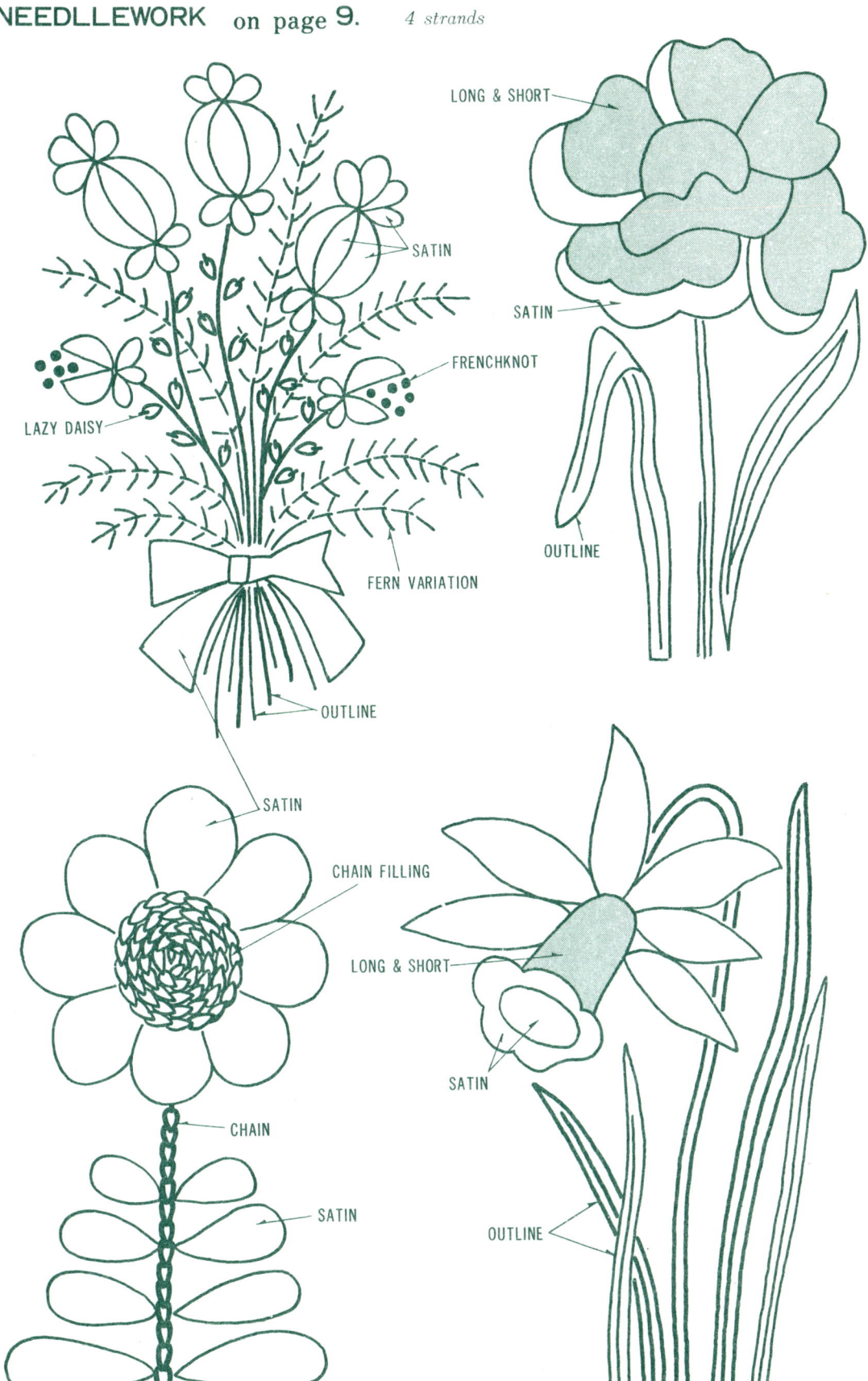

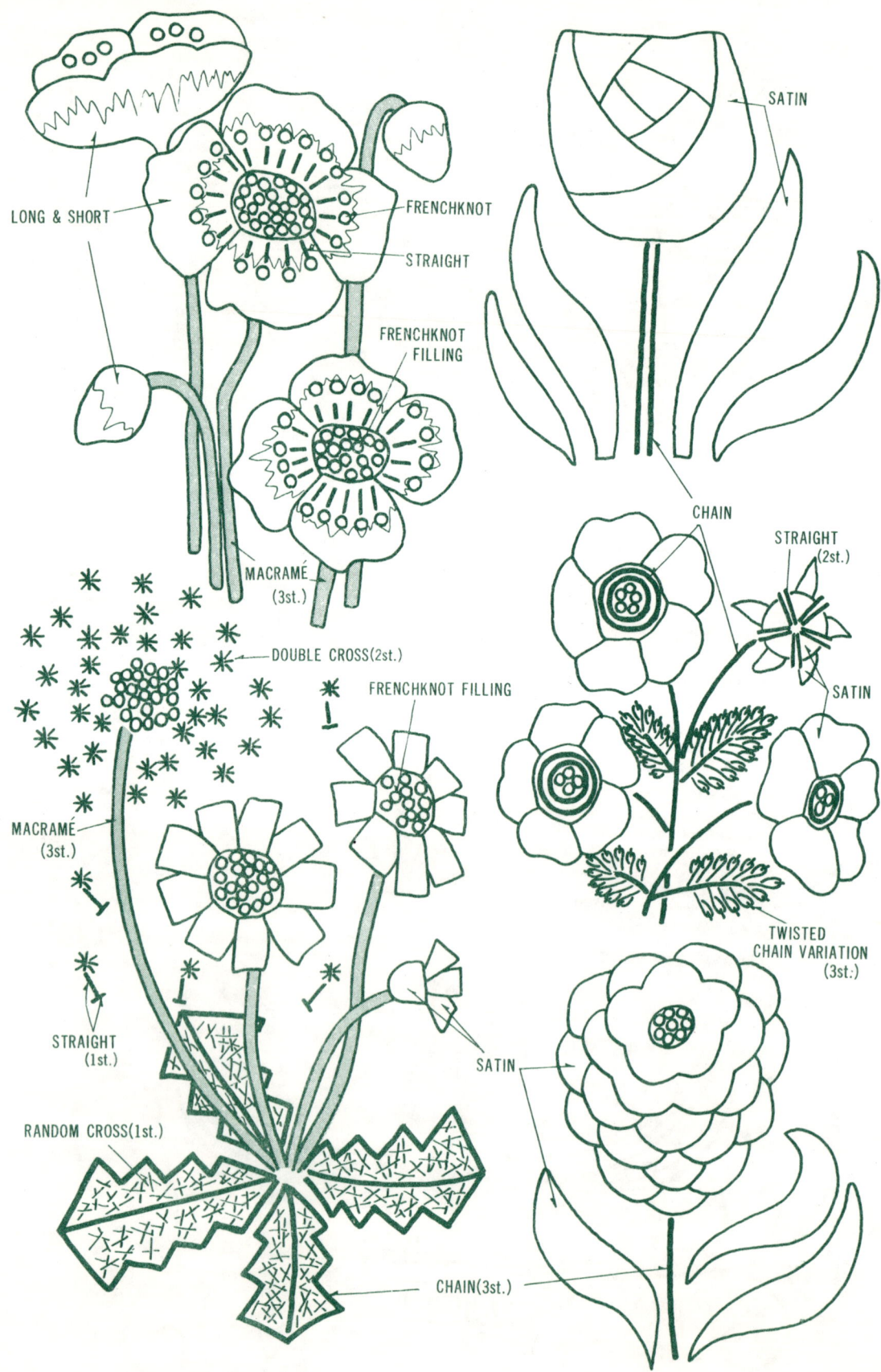

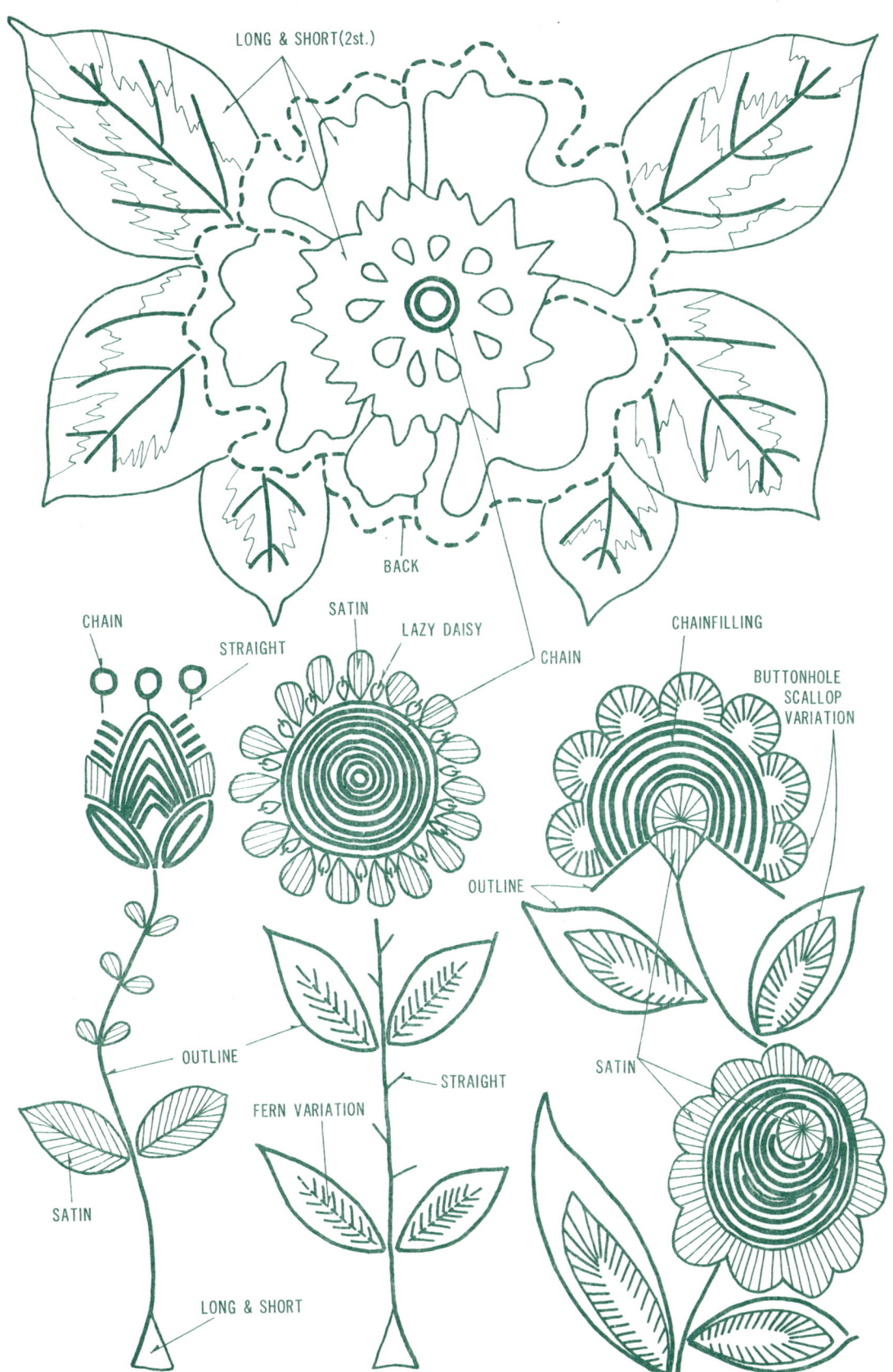

NEEDLLEWORK on page 14. *3 strands except appointment.*

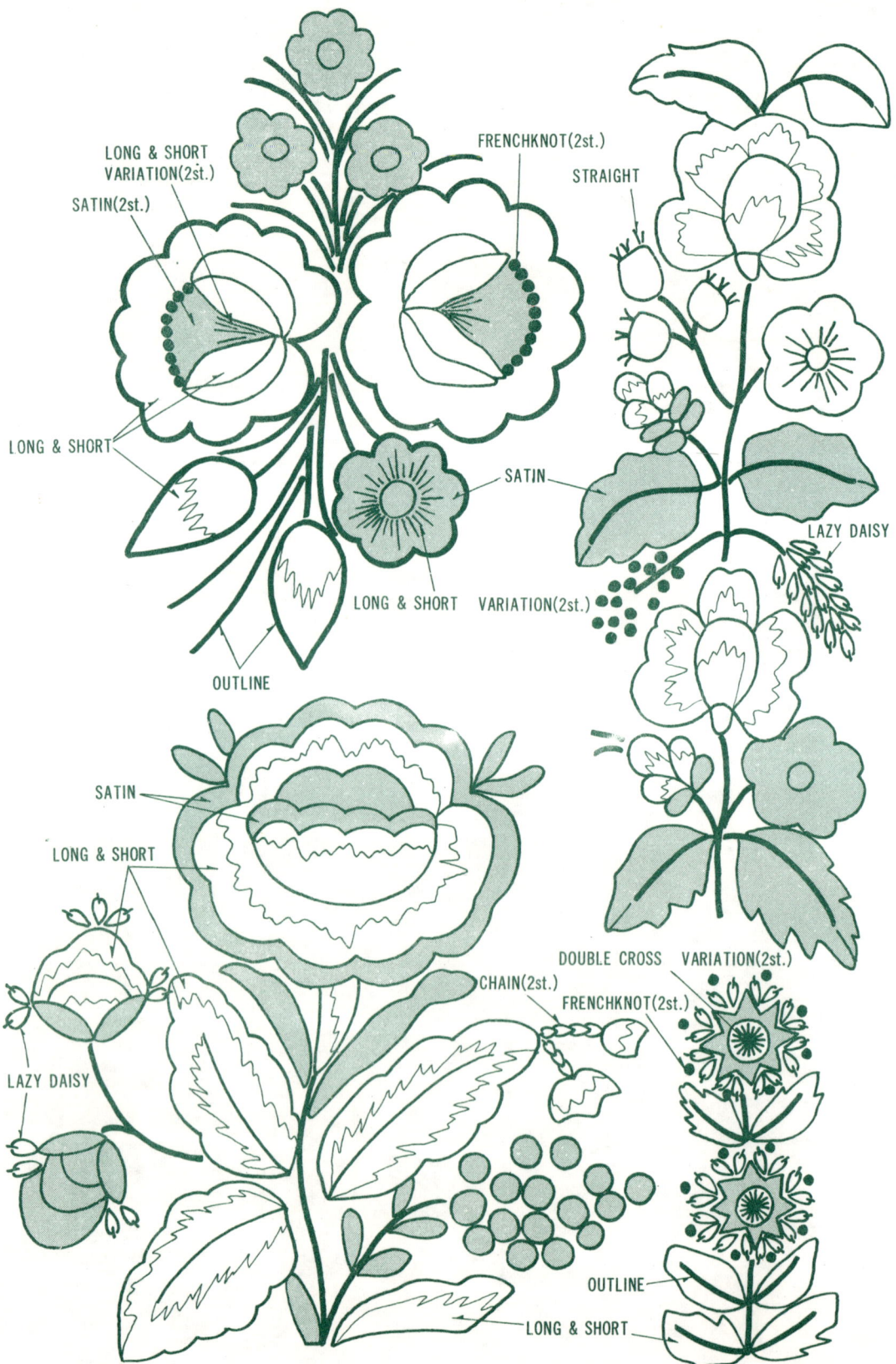

NEEDLLEWORK on page 15. *3 strands.*

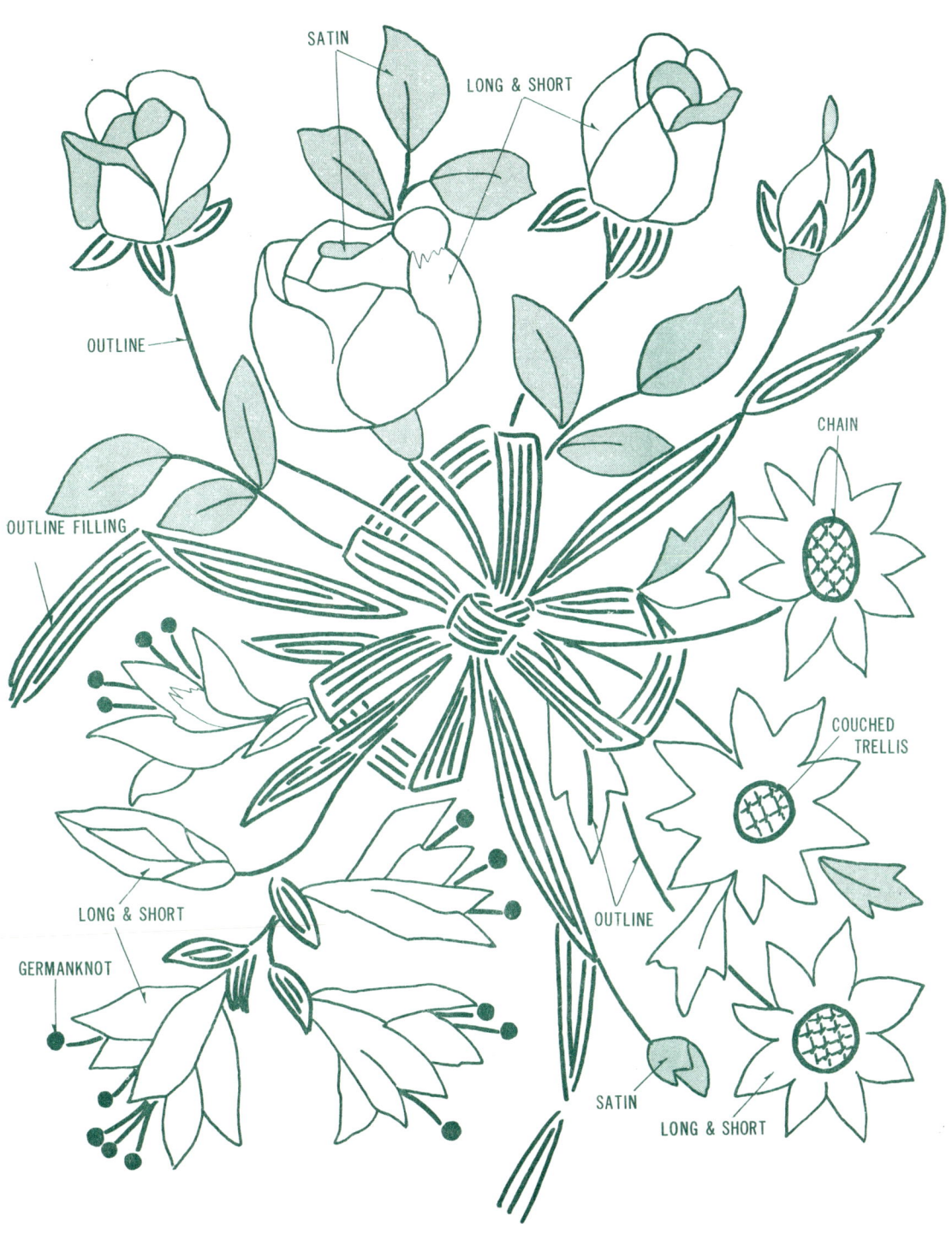

NEEDLLEWORK on page 16. *3 strands except appointment.*

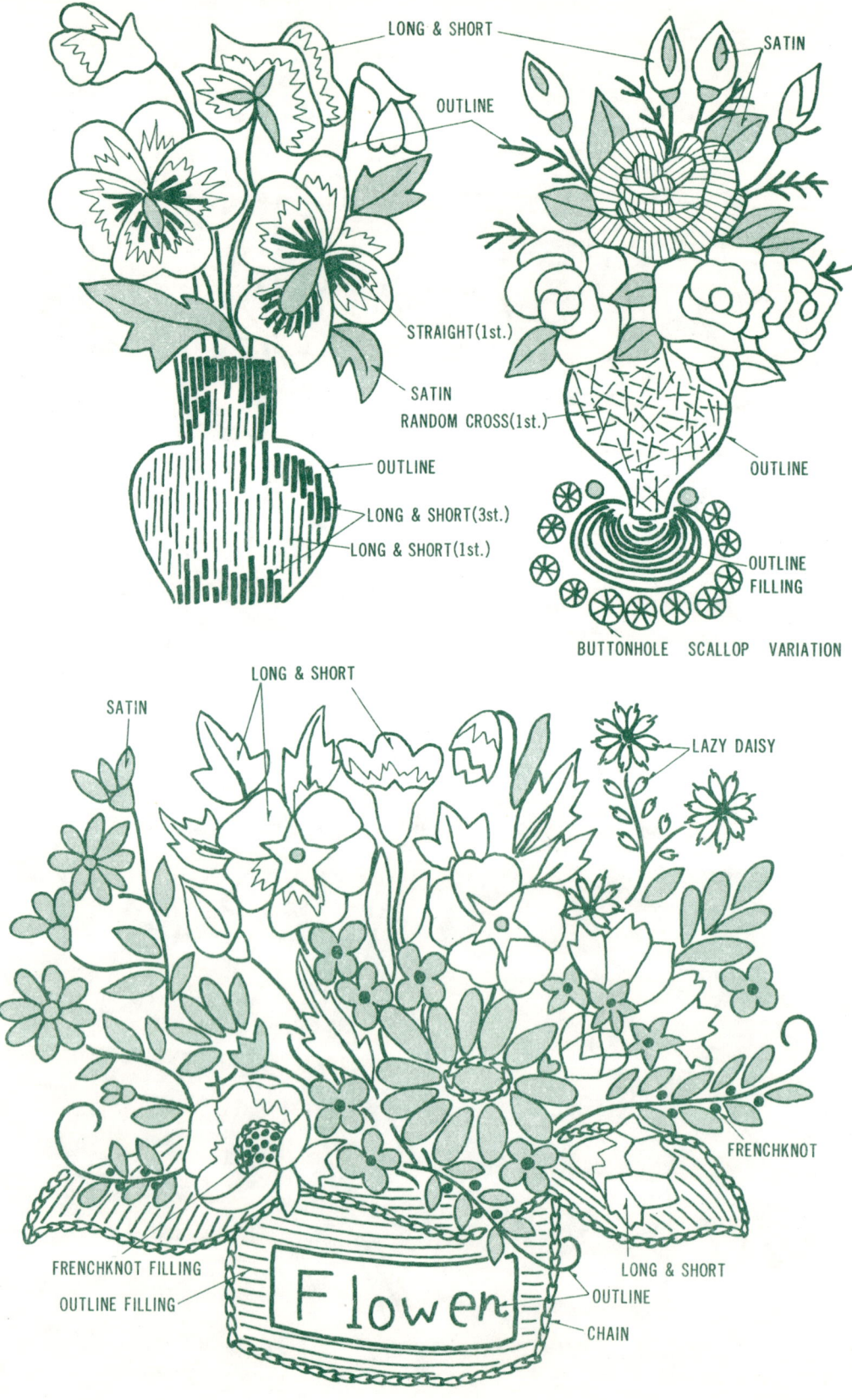

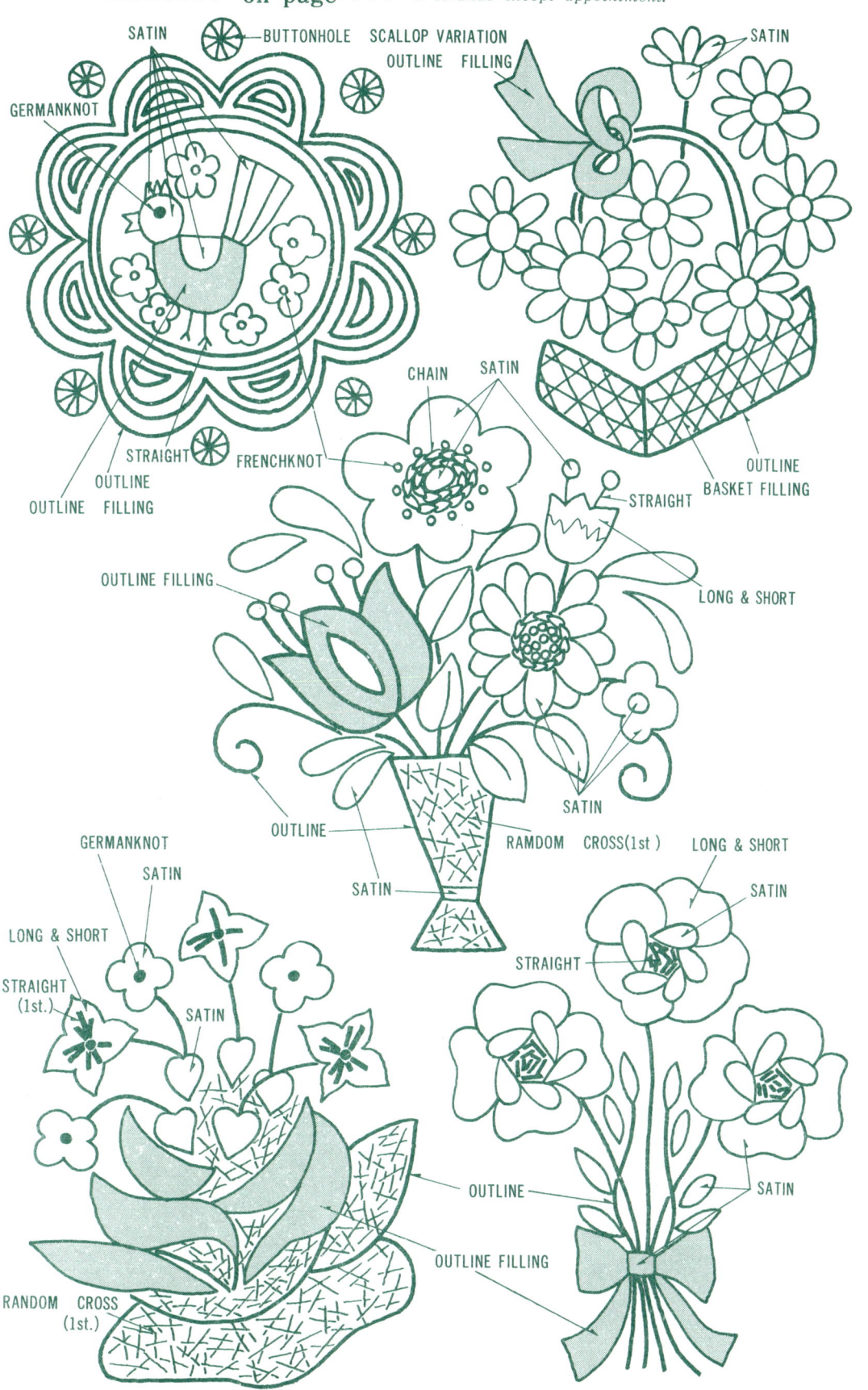

NEEDLLEWORK on page 18. *2 strands except appointment.*

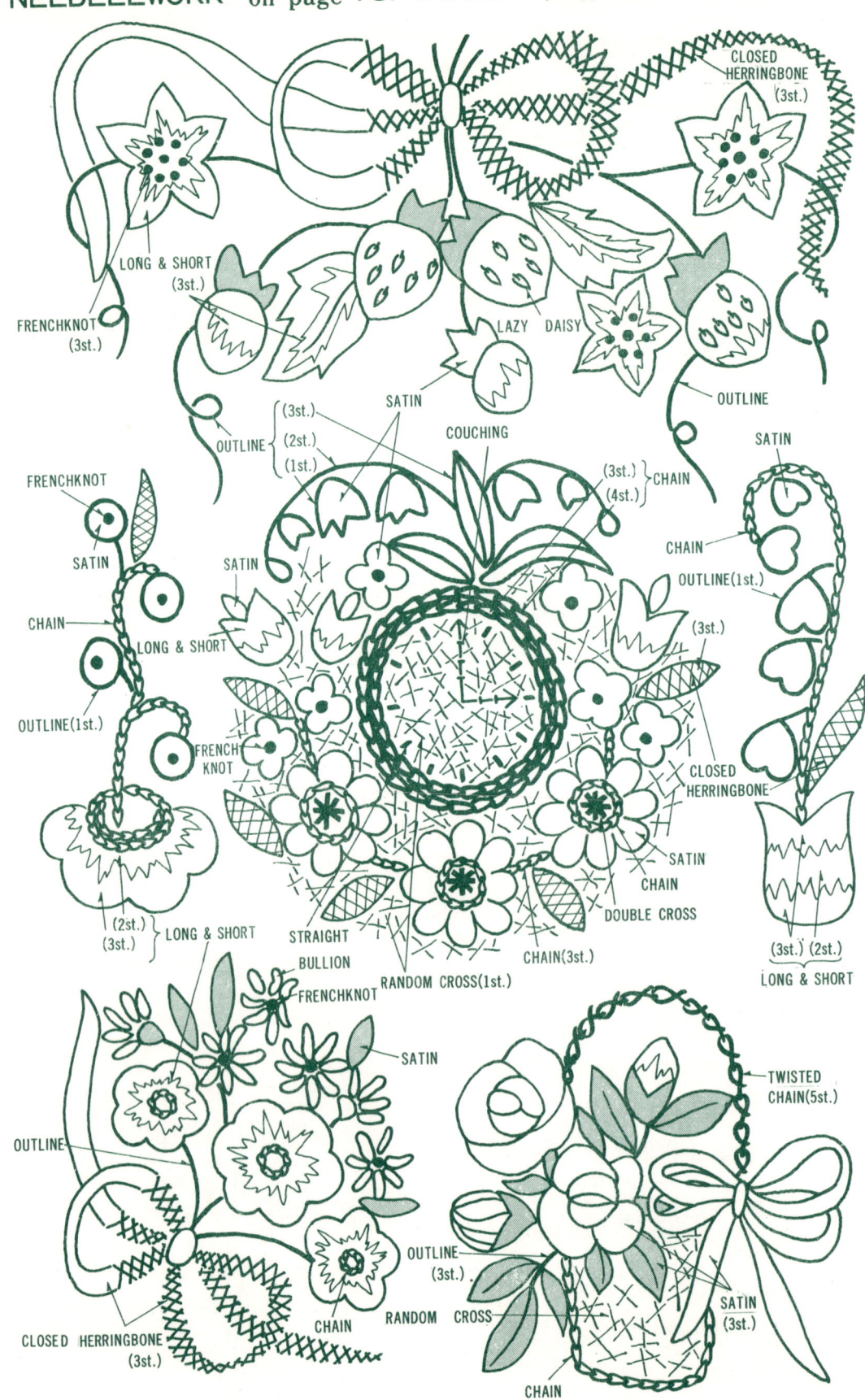

NEEDLLEWORK on page 19. *3 strands except appointment.*

NEEDLLEWORK on page 21. *2 strands except appointment.*

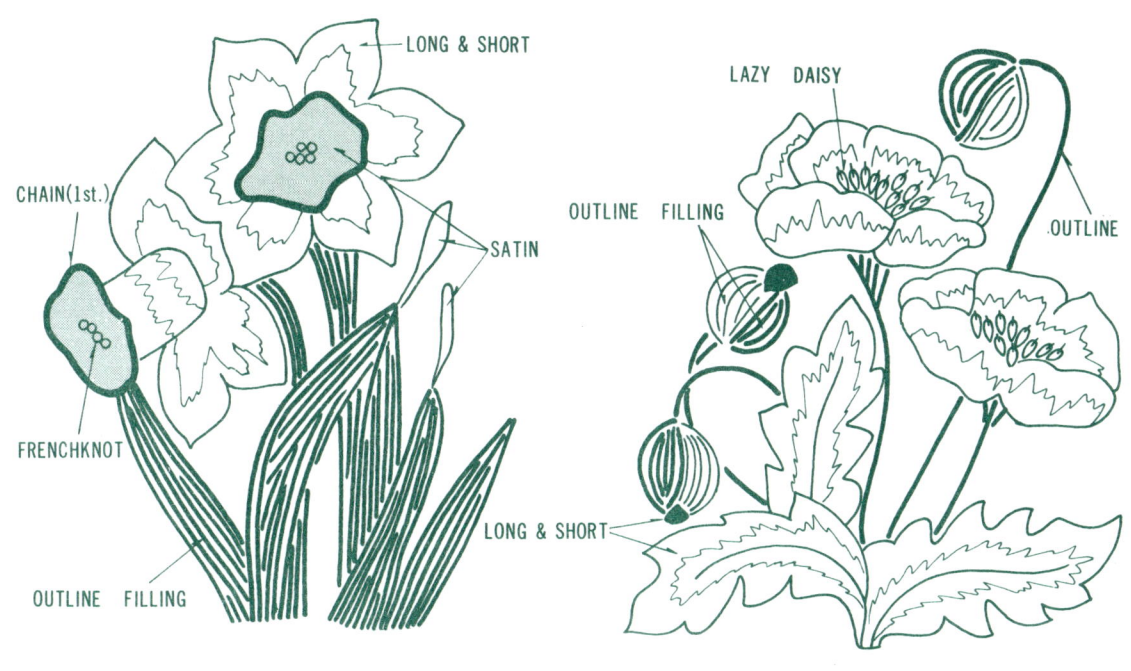

NEEDLLEWORK on page 22. *4 strands except appointment.*

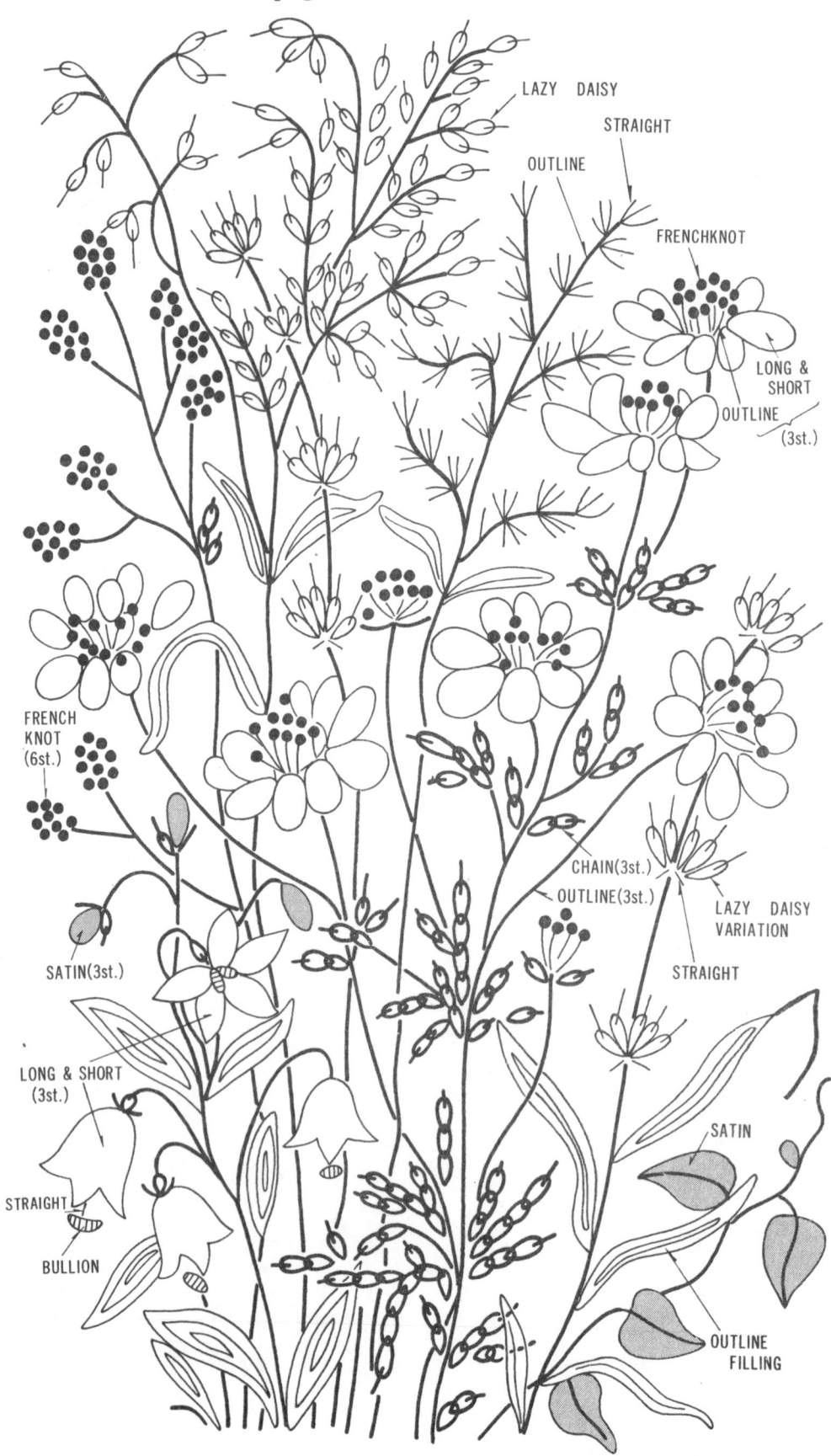

NEEDLLEWORK on page 23. *3 strands except appointment.*

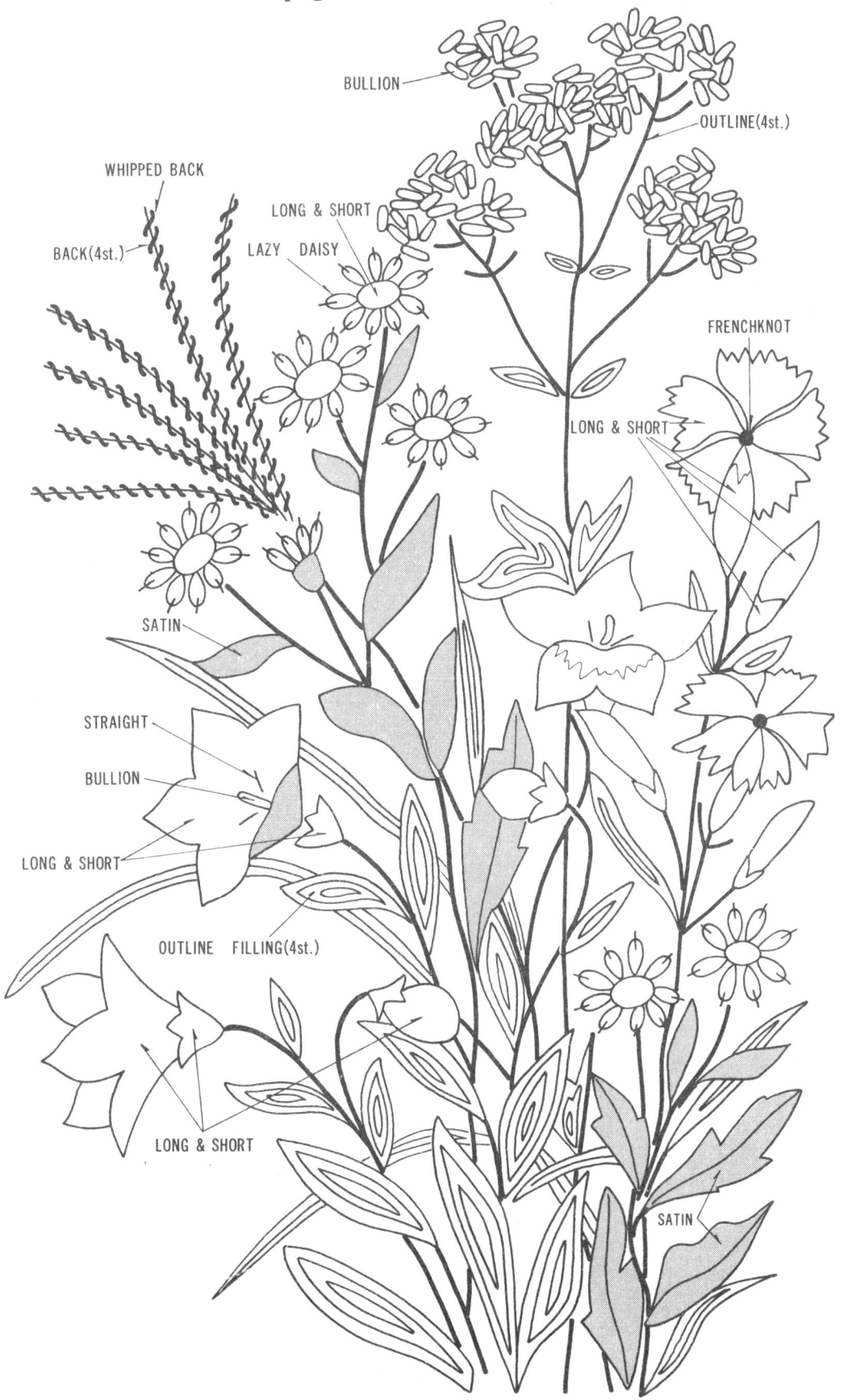

NEEDLLEWORK on page 24. *1 strand except appointment.*

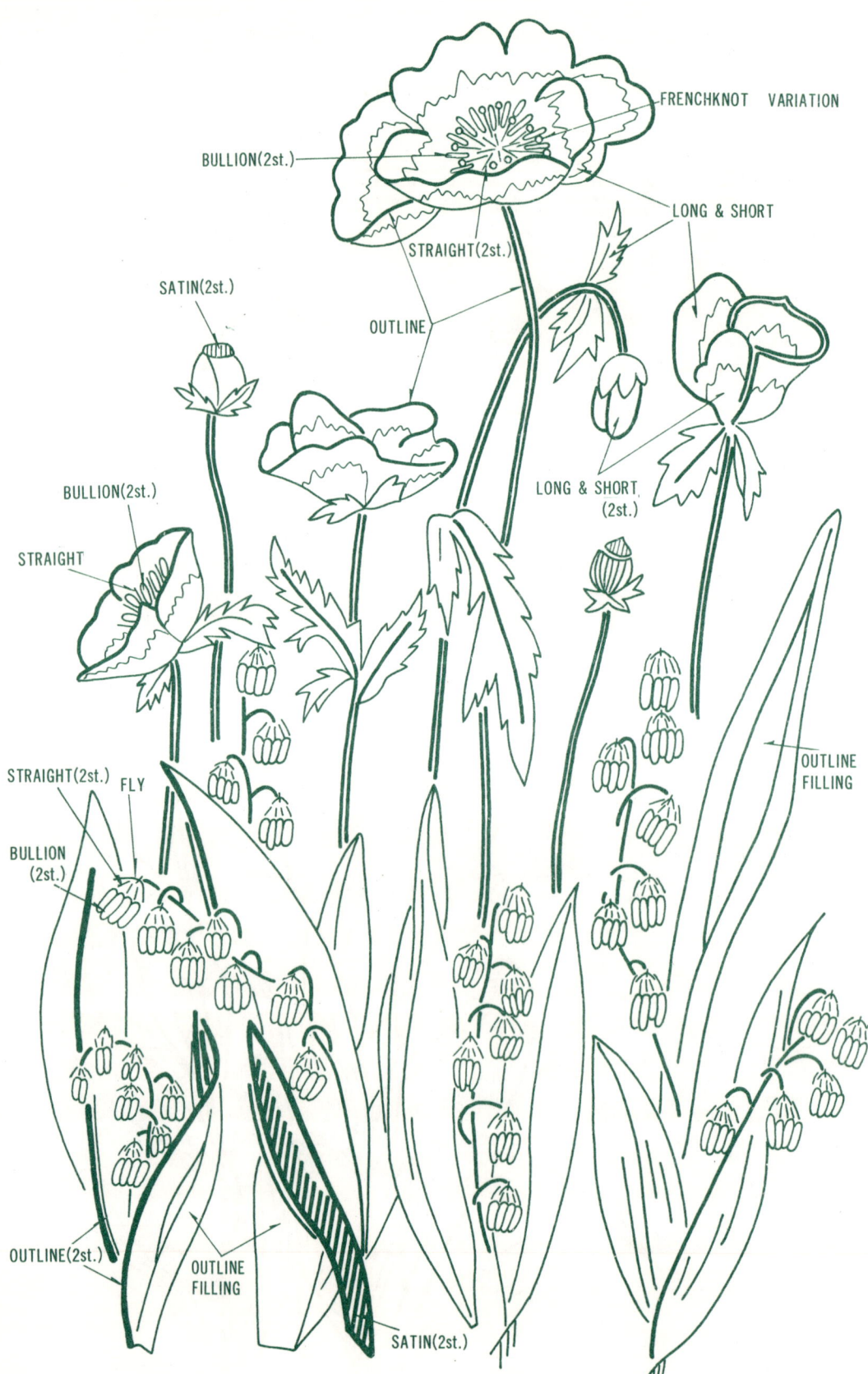

NEEDLLEWORK on page 25. *1 strands except appointment.*

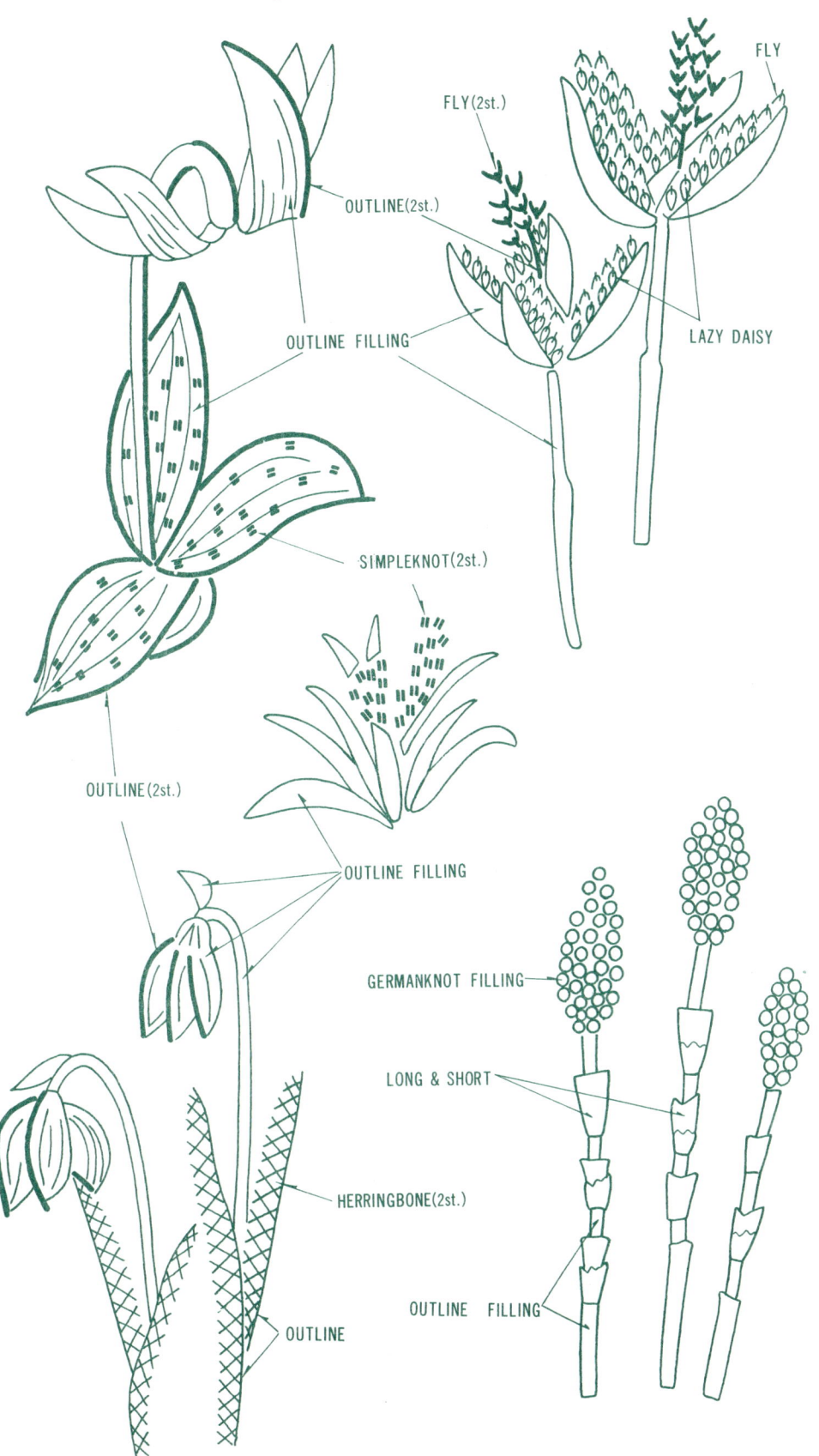

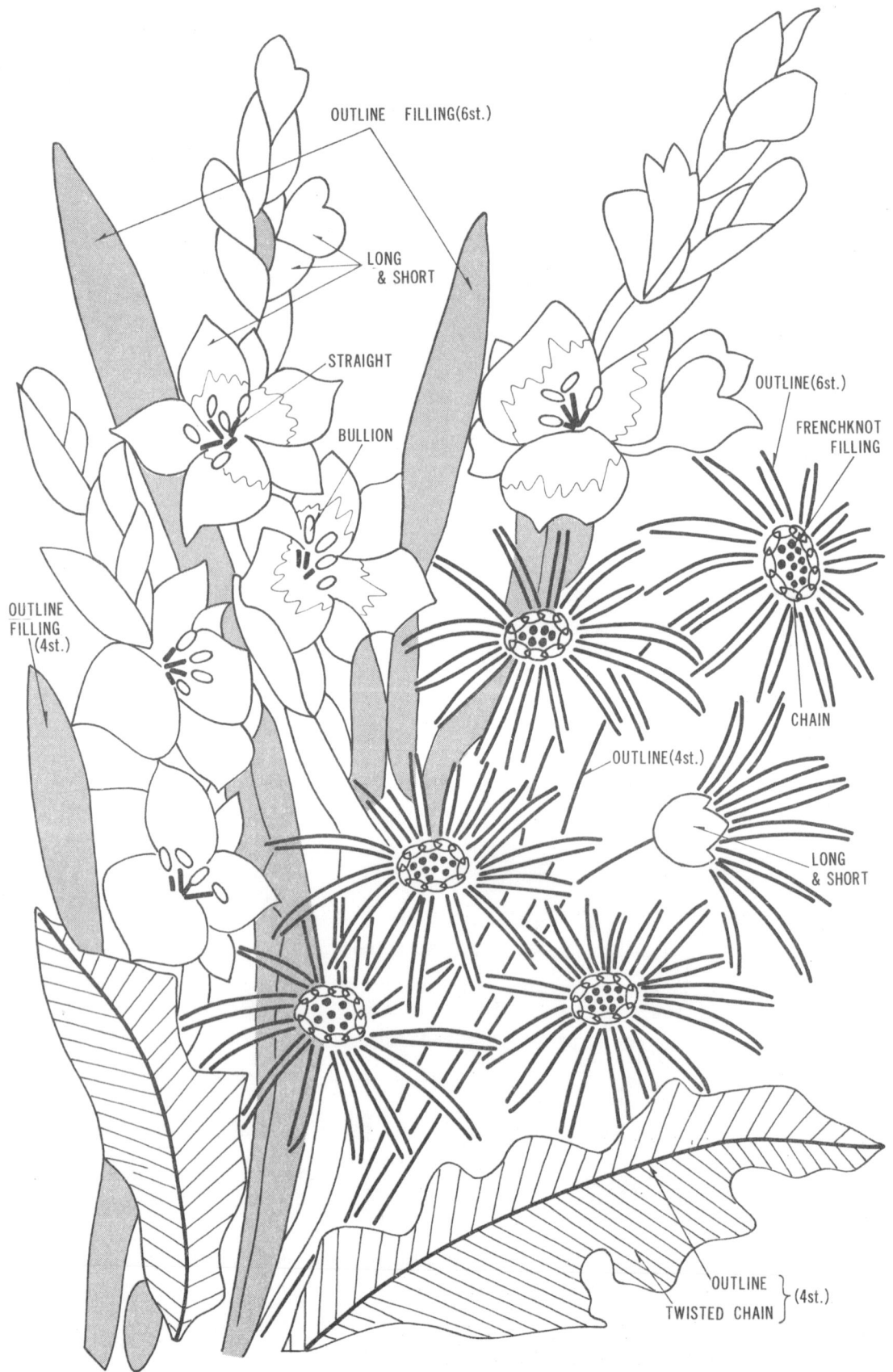

NEEDLLEWORK on page 27. *4 strands except appointment.*

- FLY(6st.)
- LONG & SHORT
- OUTLINE
- FRENCHKNOT (6st.)
- FERN VARIATION
- LONG & SHORT (3st.)
- FISHBONE
- BULLION
- SATIN (3st.)
- SATIN (3st.)
- FRENCH KNOT FILLING
- LAZY DAISY (6st.)
- LONG & SHORT
- SINGLEKNOT (6st.)

67

NEEDLLEWORK on page 29. *2 strands except appointment.*

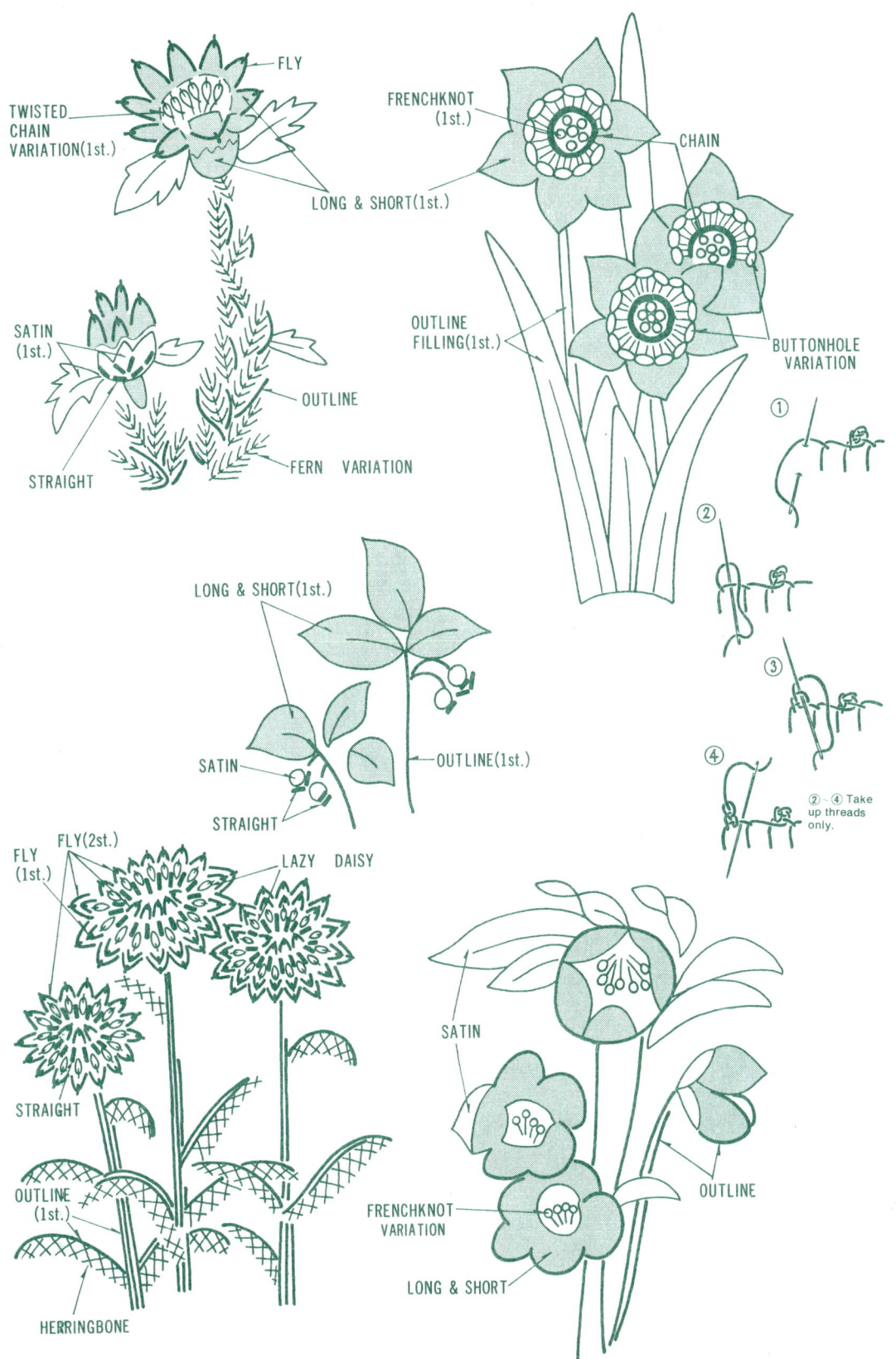

NEEDLLEWORK on page 30. *3 strands except appointment.*

NEEDLLEWORK on page 31. *2 strands except appointment.*

NEEDLLEWORK on page 32. *2 strands except appointment.*

d: SATIN(2st.), CHAIN, OUTLINE, SINGLE FEATHER (2st.), STRAIGHT (2st.), BULLION, COUCHED TRELLIS (2st.), OUTLINE (2st.), LONG & SHORT (2st.), DOUBLE CROSS

e: CHAIN BACK (2st.), FRENCH KNOT, LONG & SHORT VARIATION (2st.), SATIN (2st.), OUTLINE (2st.)

f: SATIN, STRAIGHT, CHAIN (2st.), CHAIN, FLY, OUTLINE (3st.), OUTLINE (2st.), SATIN

k: SATIN, SHEED FILLING, GERMAN KNOT, CLOSED HERRINGBONE, OUTLINE

n: SATIN, CHAIN FILLING, OUTLINE, OUTLINE, CLOSED HERRINGBONE

o: SATIN, FERN VARIATION, OUTLINE

s: SATIN, CHAIN, OUTLINE FILLING, CLOSED HERRINGBONE

t: LAZY DAISY VARIATION (2st.), DOUBLE CROSS, STRAIGHT, SATIN, OUTLINE

u: SATIN, STRAIGHT, OUTLINE, CHAIN (2st.)